©

Copyright 2022 - All rights reserved.

You may not reproduce, duplicate or send the contents of this book without direct written permission from the author. You cannot apply at this moment despite any circumstance blame the publisher or hold them to legal responsibility for any reparation, compensations, or monetary forfeiture owing to the the information included herein, either directly or indirectly.

Legal Notice: This book has copyright protection. You can use the book for personal purposes. However, you should not sell, use, alter, distribute, quote, take excerpts, or paraphrase in part or whole the material in this book without obtaining the author's permission first.

Disclaimer Notice: You must take note that the information in this document is for casual reading and entertainment purposes only. We have attempted to provide accurate, up-to-date, and reliable information. However, we do not express or imply guarantees of any kind. The persons who read admit that the writer is not giving legal, financial, medical, or other advice. We put this book content by sourcing various places.

Please consult a licensed professional before you try any techniques shown in this book. By going through this document, the book lover comes to an the agreement that under no situation is the author accountable for any forfeiture, direct or indirect, which they may incur because of the use of material contained in this document, including, but not limited to, — errors, omissions or inaccuracies.

Mileage Logbook

Name:	Position:
Adress:	
Mobile:	
Telephone:	
Email:	
Fax:	

Book info :

Book No.:	
Start Date:	End Date:

Notes:

_____
_____
_____
_____
_____
_____

Vehicle Mileage Logbook

Sheet no.:

Make :   Model :   Year :   License number :

DATE	PURPOSE OF TRAVEL	JOURNEY		ODOMETER READING			TOTAL MILES	
		From	To	Start	End	Distance (km)	Business	Private

Daily checks	Tires/Wheel	Wipers	Lights	Mirrors	Horn	Seatbelts	Brakes	Coupling devices
Monday								
Tuesday								
Wednesday								
Thursday								
Friday								
Saturday								
Sunday								

Fuel Input				
Date	Quantity	Unit	Mileage	Units

Notes :

Signature :

Vehicle Mileage Logbook

Sheet no.:

Make : Model : Year : License number :

DATE	PURPOSE OF TRAVEL	JOURNEY		ODOMETER READING			TOTAL MILES	
		From	To	Start	End	Distance (km)	Business	Private

Daily checks	Tires/Wheel	Wipers	Lights	Mirrors	Horn	Seatbelts	Brakes	Coupling devices
Monday								
Tuesday								
Wednesday								
Thursday								
Friday								
Saturday								
Sunday								

Fuel Input				
Date	Quantity	Unit	Mileage	Units

Notes :

Signature :

Vehicle Mileage Logbook

Sheet no.:

Make : Model : Year : License number :

DATE	PURPOSE OF TRAVEL	JOURNEY		ODOMETER READING			TOTAL MILES	
		From	To	Start	End	Distance (km)	Business	Private

Daily checks	Tires/ Wheel	Wipers	Lights	Mirrors	Horn	Seatbelts	Brakes	Coupling devices
Monday								
Tuesday								
Wednesday								
Thursday								
Friday								
Saturday								
Sunday								

Fuel Input				
Date	Quantity	Unit	Mileage	Units

Notes :

Signature :

Vehicle Mileage Logbook

Sheet no.:

Make :   Model :   Year :   License number :

DATE	PURPOSE OF TRAVEL	JOURNEY		ODOMETER READING			TOTAL MILES	
		From	To	Start	End	Distance (km)	Business	Private

Daily checks	Tires/Wheel	Wipers	Lights	Mirrors	Horn	Seatbelts	Brakes	Coupling devices
Monday								
Tuesday								
Wednesday								
Thursday								
Friday								
Saturday								
Sunday								

Fuel Input				
Date	Quantity	Unit	Mileage	Units

Notes :

Signature :

Vehicle Mileage Logbook

Sheet no.:

Make :   Model :   Year :   License number :

DATE	PURPOSE OF TRAVEL	JOURNEY		ODOMETER READING			TOTAL MILES	
		From	To	Start	End	Distance (km)	Business	Private

Daily checks	Tires/Wheel	Wipers	Lights	Mirrors	Horn	Seatbelts	Brakes	Coupling devices
Monday								
Tuesday								
Wednesday								
Thursday								
Friday								
Saturday								
Sunday								

Fuel Input				
Date	Quantity	Unit	Mileage	Units

Notes :

Signature :

Vehicle Mileage Logbook

Sheet no.:

Make :   Model :   Year :   License number :

DATE	PURPOSE OF TRAVEL	JOURNEY		ODOMETER READING			TOTAL MILES	
		From	To	Start	End	Distance (km)	Business	Private

Daily checks	Tires/ Wheel	Wipers	Lights	Mirrors	Horn	Seatbelts	Brakes	Coupling devices
Monday								
Tuesday								
Wednesday								
Thursday								
Friday								
Saturday								
Sunday								

Fuel Input				
Date	Quantity	Unit	Mileage	Units

Notes :

Signature :

Vehicle Mileage Logbook

Sheet no.:

Make :　　　　Model :　　　　Year :　　　　License number :

DATE	PURPOSE OF TRAVEL	JOURNEY		ODOMETER READING			TOTAL MILES	
		From	To	Start	End	Distance (km)	Business	Private

Daily checks	Tires/Wheel	Wipers	Lights	Mirrors	Horn	Seatbelts	Brakes	Coupling devices
Monday								
Tuesday								
Wednesday								
Thursday								
Friday								
Saturday								
Sunday								

Fuel Input				
Date	Quantity	Unit	Mileage	Units

Notes :

Signature :

Vehicle Mileage Logbook

Sheet no.:

Make :　　Model :　　Year :　　License number :

DATE	PURPOSE OF TRAVEL	JOURNEY		ODOMETER READING			TOTAL MILES	
		From	To	Start	End	Distance (km)	Business	Private

Daily checks	Tires/Wheel	Wipers	Lights	Mirrors	Horn	Seatbelts	Brakes	Coupling devices
Monday								
Tuesday								
Wednesday								
Thursday								
Friday								
Saturday								
Sunday								

Fuel Input

Date	Quantity	Unit	Mileage	Units

Notes :

Signature :

Vehicle Mileage Logbook

Sheet no.:

Make :　　　Model :　　　Year :　　　License number :

DATE	PURPOSE OF TRAVEL	JOURNEY		ODOMETER READING			TOTAL MILES	
		From	To	Start	End	Distance (km)	Business	Private

Daily checks	Tires/Wheel	Wipers	Lights	Mirrors	Horn	Seatbelts	Brakes	Coupling devices
Monday								
Tuesday								
Wednesday								
Thursday								
Friday								
Saturday								
Sunday								

Fuel Input				
Date	Quantity	Unit	Mileage	Units

Notes :

Signature :

Vehicle Mileage Logbook

Sheet no.:

Make : Model : Year : License number :

DATE	PURPOSE OF TRAVEL	JOURNEY		ODOMETER READING			TOTAL MILES	
		From	To	Start	End	Distance (km)	Business	Private

Daily checks	Tires/Wheel	Wipers	Lights	Mirrors	Horn	Seatbelts	Brakes	Coupling devices
Monday								
Tuesday								
Wednesday								
Thursday								
Friday								
Saturday								
Sunday								

Fuel Input				
Date	Quantity	Unit	Mileage	Units

Notes :

Signature :

Vehicle Mileage Logbook

Sheet no.:

Make :   Model :   Year :   License number :

DATE	PURPOSE OF TRAVEL	JOURNEY		ODOMETER READING			TOTAL MILES	
		From	To	Start	End	Distance (km)	Business	Private

Daily checks	Tires/Wheel	Wipers	Lights	Mirrors	Horn	Seatbelts	Brakes	Coupling devices
Monday								
Tuesday								
Wednesday								
Thursday								
Friday								
Saturday								
Sunday								

Fuel Input				
Date	Quantity	Unit	Mileage	Units

Notes :

Signature :

Vehicle Mileage Logbook

Sheet no.:

Make :   Model :   Year :   License number :

DATE	PURPOSE OF TRAVEL	JOURNEY		ODOMETER READING			TOTAL MILES	
		From	To	Start	End	Distance (km)	Business	Private

Daily checks	Tires/Wheel	Wipers	Lights	Mirrors	Horn	Seatbelts	Brakes	Coupling devices
Monday								
Tuesday								
Wednesday								
Thursday								
Friday								
Saturday								
Sunday								

Fuel Input				
Date	Quantity	Unit	Mileage	Units

Notes :

Signature :

Vehicle Mileage Logbook

Sheet no.:

Make :　　　　　Model :　　　　　　　　Year :　　　　License number :

DATE	PURPOSE OF TRAVEL	JOURNEY		ODOMETER READING			TOTAL MILES	
		From	To	Start	End	Distance (km)	Business	Private

Daily checks	Tires/Wheel	Wipers	Lights	Mirrors	Horn	Seatbelts	Brakes	Coupling devices
Monday								
Tuesday								
Wednesday								
Thursday								
Friday								
Saturday								
Sunday								

Fuel Input				
Date	Quantity	Unit	Mileage	Units

Notes :

Signature :

Vehicle Mileage Logbook

Sheet no.:

Make :   Model :   Year :   License number :

DATE	PURPOSE OF TRAVEL	JOURNEY		ODOMETER READING			TOTAL MILES	
		From	To	Start	End	Distance (km)	Business	Private

Daily checks	Tires/Wheel	Wipers	Lights	Mirrors	Horn	Seatbelts	Brakes	Coupling devices
Monday								
Tuesday								
Wednesday								
Thursday								
Friday								
Saturday								
Sunday								

Fuel Input

Date	Quantity	Unit	Mileage	Units

Notes :
_____
_____
_____
_____
_____

Signature :

Vehicle Mileage Logbook

Sheet no.:

Make :   Model :   Year :   License number :

DATE	PURPOSE OF TRAVEL	JOURNEY		ODOMETER READING			TOTAL MILES	
		From	To	Start	End	Distance (km)	Business	Private

Daily checks	Tires/Wheel	Wipers	Lights	Mirrors	Horn	Seatbelts	Brakes	Coupling devices
Monday								
Tuesday								
Wednesday								
Thursday								
Friday								
Saturday								
Sunday								

Fuel Input				
Date	Quantity	Unit	Mileage	Units

Notes :

Signature :

Vehicle Mileage Logbook

Sheet no.:

Make :　　Model :　　Year :　　License number :

DATE	PURPOSE OF TRAVEL	JOURNEY		ODOMETER READING			TOTAL MILES	
		From	To	Start	End	Distance (km)	Business	Private

Daily checks	Tires/Wheel	Wipers	Lights	Mirrors	Horn	Seatbelts	Brakes	Coupling devices
Monday								
Tuesday								
Wednesday								
Thursday								
Friday								
Saturday								
Sunday								

Fuel Input				
Date	Quantity	Unit	Mileage	Units

Notes :

Signature :

Vehicle Mileage Logbook

Sheet no.:

Make :　　　　Model :　　　　Year :　　　　License number :

DATE	PURPOSE OF TRAVEL	JOURNEY		ODOMETER READING			TOTAL MILES	
		From	To	Start	End	Distance (km)	Business	Private

Daily checks	Tires/Wheel	Wipers	Lights	Mirrors	Horn	Seatbelts	Brakes	Coupling devices
Monday								
Tuesday								
Wednesday								
Thursday								
Friday								
Saturday								
Sunday								

Fuel Input				
Date	Quantity	Unit	Mileage	Units

Notes :

Signature :

Vehicle Mileage Logbook

Sheet no.:

Make : Model : Year : License number :

DATE	PURPOSE OF TRAVEL	JOURNEY		ODOMETER READING			TOTAL MILES	
		From	To	Start	End	Distance (km)	Business	Private

Daily checks	Tires/Wheel	Wipers	Lights	Mirrors	Horn	Seatbelts	Brakes	Coupling devices
Monday								
Tuesday								
Wednesday								
Thursday								
Friday								
Saturday								
Sunday								

Fuel Input				
Date	Quantity	Unit	Mileage	Units

Notes :

Signature :

Vehicle Mileage Logbook

Sheet no.:

Make : Model : Year : License number :

DATE	PURPOSE OF TRAVEL	JOURNEY		ODOMETER READING			TOTAL MILES	
		From	To	Start	End	Distance (km)	Business	Private

Daily checks	Tires/Wheel	Wipers	Lights	Mirrors	Horn	Seatbelts	Brakes	Coupling devices
Monday								
Tuesday								
Wednesday								
Thursday								
Friday								
Saturday								
Sunday								

Fuel Input

Date	Quantity	Unit	Mileage	Units

Notes :

Signature :

Vehicle Mileage Logbook

Sheet no.:

Make :　　　Model :　　　Year :　　　License number :

DATE	PURPOSE OF TRAVEL	JOURNEY		ODOMETER READING			TOTAL MILES	
		From	To	Start	End	Distance (km)	Business	Private

Daily checks	Tires/Wheel	Wipers	Lights	Mirrors	Horn	Seatbelts	Brakes	Coupling devices
Monday								
Tuesday								
Wednesday								
Thursday								
Friday								
Saturday								
Sunday								

Fuel Input

Date	Quantity	Unit	Mileage	Units

Notes :

Signature :

Vehicle Mileage Logbook

Sheet no.:

Make :　　　Model :　　　Year :　　　License number :

DATE	PURPOSE OF TRAVEL	JOURNEY		ODOMETER READING			TOTAL MILES	
		From	To	Start	End	Distance (km)	Business	Private

Daily checks	Tires/ Wheel	Wipers	Lights	Mirrors	Horn	Seatbelts	Brakes	Coupling devices
Monday								
Tuesday								
Wednesday								
Thursday								
Friday								
Saturday								
Sunday								

Fuel Input				
Date	Quantity	Unit	Mileage	Units

Notes :

Signature :

Vehicle Mileage Logbook

Sheet no.:

Make :   Model :   Year :   License number :

DATE	PURPOSE OF TRAVEL	JOURNEY		ODOMETER READING			TOTAL MILES	
		From	To	Start	End	Distance (km)	Business	Private

Daily checks	Tires/ Wheel	Wipers	Lights	Mirrors	Horn	Seatbelts	Brakes	Coupling devices
Monday								
Tuesday								
Wednesday								
Thursday								
Friday								
Saturday								
Sunday								

Fuel Input				
Date	Quantity	Unit	Mileage	Units

Notes :

Signature :

Vehicle Mileage Logbook

Sheet no.:

Make : Model : Year : License number :

DATE	PURPOSE OF TRAVEL	JOURNEY		ODOMETER READING			TOTAL MILES	
		From	To	Start	End	Distance (km)	Business	Private

Daily checks	Tires/ Wheel	Wipers	Lights	Mirrors	Horn	Seatbelts	Brakes	Coupling devices
Monday								
Tuesday								
Wednesday								
Thursday								
Friday								
Saturday								
Sunday								

Fuel Input				
Date	Quantity	Unit	Mileage	Units

Notes :

Signature :

Vehicle Mileage Logbook

Sheet no.:

Make :　　　　Model :　　　　Year :　　　　License number :

DATE	PURPOSE OF TRAVEL	JOURNEY		ODOMETER READING			TOTAL MILES	
		From	To	Start	End	Distance (km)	Business	Private

Daily checks	Tires/Wheel	Wipers	Lights	Mirrors	Horn	Seatbelts	Brakes	Coupling devices
Monday								
Tuesday								
Wednesday								
Thursday								
Friday								
Saturday								
Sunday								

Fuel Input				
Date	Quantity	Unit	Mileage	Units

Notes :

_____
_____
_____
_____
_____

Signature :

Vehicle Mileage Logbook

Sheet no.:

Make :　　　　Model :　　　　Year :　　　　License number :

DATE	PURPOSE OF TRAVEL	JOURNEY		ODOMETER READING			TOTAL MILES	
		From	To	Start	End	Distance (km)	Business	Private

Daily checks	Tires/ Wheel	Wipers	Lights	Mirrors	Horn	Seatbelts	Brakes	Coupling devices
Monday								
Tuesday								
Wednesday								
Thursday								
Friday								
Saturday								
Sunday								

Fuel Input				
Date	Quantity	Unit	Mileage	Units

Notes :

_____
_____
_____
_____
_____
_____
_____

Signature :

Vehicle Mileage Logbook

Sheet no.:

Make : Model : Year : License number :

DATE	PURPOSE OF TRAVEL	JOURNEY		ODOMETER READING			TOTAL MILES	
		From	To	Start	End	Distance (km)	Business	Private

Daily checks	Tires/Wheel	Wipers	Lights	Mirrors	Horn	Seatbelts	Brakes	Coupling devices
Monday								
Tuesday								
Wednesday								
Thursday								
Friday								
Saturday								
Sunday								

Fuel Input				
Date	Quantity	Unit	Mileage	Units

Notes :

Signature :

Vehicle Mileage Logbook

Sheet no.:

Make :   Model :   Year :   License number :

DATE	PURPOSE OF TRAVEL	JOURNEY		ODOMETER READING			TOTAL MILES	
		From	To	Start	End	Distance (km)	Business	Private

Daily checks	Tires/Wheel	Wipers	Lights	Mirrors	Horn	Seatbelts	Brakes	Coupling devices
Monday								
Tuesday								
Wednesday								
Thursday								
Friday								
Saturday								
Sunday								

Fuel Input				
Date	Quantity	Unit	Mileage	Units

Notes :

Signature :

Vehicle Mileage Logbook

Sheet no.:

Make : Model : Year : License number :

DATE	PURPOSE OF TRAVEL	JOURNEY		ODOMETER READING			TOTAL MILES	
		From	To	Start	End	Distance (km)	Business	Private

Daily checks	Tires/Wheel	Wipers	Lights	Mirrors	Horn	Seatbelts	Brakes	Coupling devices
Monday								
Tuesday								
Wednesday								
Thursday								
Friday								
Saturday								
Sunday								

Fuel Input

Date	Quantity	Unit	Mileage	Units

Notes :

Signature :

Vehicle Mileage Logbook

Sheet no.:

Make :　　Model :　　Year :　　License number :

DATE	PURPOSE OF TRAVEL	JOURNEY		ODOMETER READING			TOTAL MILES	
		From	To	Start	End	Distance (km)	Business	Private

Daily checks	Tires/Wheel	Wipers	Lights	Mirrors	Horn	Seatbelts	Brakes	Coupling devices
Monday								
Tuesday								
Wednesday								
Thursday								
Friday								
Saturday								
Sunday								

Fuel Input				
Date	Quantity	Unit	Mileage	Units

Notes :

Signature :

Vehicle Mileage Logbook

Sheet no.:

Make :　　　　Model :　　　　Year :　　　　License number :

DATE	PURPOSE OF TRAVEL	JOURNEY		ODOMETER READING			TOTAL MILES	
		From	To	Start	End	Distance (km)	Business	Private

Daily checks	Tires/Wheel	Wipers	Lights	Mirrors	Horn	Seatbelts	Brakes	Coupling devices
Monday								
Tuesday								
Wednesday								
Thursday								
Friday								
Saturday								
Sunday								

Fuel Input				
Date	Quantity	Unit	Mileage	Units

Notes :
_____
_____
_____
_____
_____

Signature :

Vehicle Mileage Logbook

Sheet no.:

Make :   Model :   Year :   License number :

DATE	PURPOSE OF TRAVEL	JOURNEY		ODOMETER READING			TOTAL MILES	
		From	To	Start	End	Distance (km)	Business	Private

Daily checks	Tires/Wheel	Wipers	Lights	Mirrors	Horn	Seatbelts	Brakes	Coupling devices
Monday								
Tuesday								
Wednesday								
Thursday								
Friday								
Saturday								
Sunday								

Fuel Input				
Date	Quantity	Unit	Mileage	Units

Notes :

Signature :

Vehicle Mileage Logbook

Sheet no.:

Make : Model : Year : License number :

DATE	PURPOSE OF TRAVEL	JOURNEY		ODOMETER READING			TOTAL MILES	
		From	To	Start	End	Distance (km)	Business	Private

Daily checks	Tires/Wheel	Wipers	Lights	Mirrors	Horn	Seatbelts	Brakes	Coupling devices
Monday								
Tuesday								
Wednesday								
Thursday								
Friday								
Saturday								
Sunday								

Fuel Input				
Date	Quantity	Unit	Mileage	Units

Notes :

Signature :

Vehicle Mileage Logbook

Sheet no.:

Make :   Model :   Year :   License number :

DATE	PURPOSE OF TRAVEL	JOURNEY		ODOMETER READING			TOTAL MILES	
		From	To	Start	End	Distance (km)	Business	Private

Daily checks	Tires/Wheel	Wipers	Lights	Mirrors	Horn	Seatbelts	Brakes	Coupling devices
Monday								
Tuesday								
Wednesday								
Thursday								
Friday								
Saturday								
Sunday								

Fuel Input				
Date	Quantity	Unit	Mileage	Units

Notes :

Signature :

Vehicle Mileage Logbook

Sheet no.:

Make :   Model :   Year :   License number :

DATE	PURPOSE OF TRAVEL	JOURNEY		ODOMETER READING			TOTAL MILES	
		From	To	Start	End	Distance (km)	Business	Private

Daily checks	Tires/ Wheel	Wipers	Lights	Mirrors	Horn	Seatbelts	Brakes	Coupling devices
Monday								
Tuesday								
Wednesday								
Thursday								
Friday								
Saturday								
Sunday								

Fuel Input				
Date	Quantity	Unit	Mileage	Units

Notes :

_____
_____
_____
_____
_____
_____

Signature :

Vehicle Mileage Logbook

Sheet no.:

Make : Model : Year : License number :

DATE	PURPOSE OF TRAVEL	JOURNEY		ODOMETER READING			TOTAL MILES	
		From	To	Start	End	Distance (km)	Business	Private

Daily checks	Tires/Wheel	Wipers	Lights	Mirrors	Horn	Seatbelts	Brakes	Coupling devices
Monday								
Tuesday								
Wednesday								
Thursday								
Friday								
Saturday								
Sunday								

Fuel Input				
Date	Quantity	Unit	Mileage	Units

Notes :

Signature :

Vehicle Mileage Logbook

Sheet no.:

Make :　　　　Model :　　　　Year :　　　　License number :

DATE	PURPOSE OF TRAVEL	JOURNEY		ODOMETER READING			TOTAL MILES	
		From	To	Start	End	Distance (km)	Business	Private

Daily checks	Tires/Wheel	Wipers	Lights	Mirrors	Horn	Seatbelts	Brakes	Coupling devices
Monday								
Tuesday								
Wednesday								
Thursday								
Friday								
Saturday								
Sunday								

Fuel Input				
Date	Quantity	Unit	Mileage	Units

Notes :

Signature :

Vehicle Mileage Logbook

Sheet no.:

Make :　　　Model :　　　Year :　　　License number :

DATE	PURPOSE OF TRAVEL	JOURNEY		ODOMETER READING			TOTAL MILES	
		From	To	Start	End	Distance (km)	Business	Private

Daily checks	Tires/Wheel	Wipers	Lights	Mirrors	Horn	Seatbelts	Brakes	Coupling devices
Monday								
Tuesday								
Wednesday								
Thursday								
Friday								
Saturday								
Sunday								

Fuel Input				
Date	Quantity	Unit	Mileage	Units

Notes :

Signature :

Vehicle Mileage Logbook

Sheet no.:

Make :   Model :   Year :   License number :

DATE	PURPOSE OF TRAVEL	JOURNEY		ODOMETER READING			TOTAL MILES	
		From	To	Start	End	Distance (km)	Business	Private

Daily checks	Tires/Wheel	Wipers	Lights	Mirrors	Horn	Seatbelts	Brakes	Coupling devices
Monday								
Tuesday								
Wednesday								
Thursday								
Friday								
Saturday								
Sunday								

Fuel Input				
Date	Quantity	Unit	Mileage	Units

Notes :

Signature :

Vehicle Mileage Logbook

Sheet no.:

Make : Model : Year : License number :

DATE	PURPOSE OF TRAVEL	JOURNEY		ODOMETER READING			TOTAL MILES	
		From	To	Start	End	Distance (km)	Business	Private

Daily checks	Tires/Wheel	Wipers	Lights	Mirrors	Horn	Seatbelts	Brakes	Coupling devices
Monday								
Tuesday								
Wednesday								
Thursday								
Friday								
Saturday								
Sunday								

Fuel Input				
Date	Quantity	Unit	Mileage	Units

Notes :

Signature :

Vehicle Mileage Logbook

Sheet no.:

Make :   Model :   Year :   License number :

DATE	PURPOSE OF TRAVEL	JOURNEY		ODOMETER READING			TOTAL MILES	
		From	To	Start	End	Distance (km)	Business	Private

Daily checks	Tires/Wheel	Wipers	Lights	Mirrors	Horn	Seatbelts	Brakes	Coupling devices
Monday								
Tuesday								
Wednesday								
Thursday								
Friday								
Saturday								
Sunday								

Fuel Input				
Date	Quantity	Unit	Mileage	Units

Notes :

Signature :

Vehicle Mileage Logbook

Sheet no.:

Make : Model : Year : License number :

DATE	PURPOSE OF TRAVEL	JOURNEY		ODOMETER READING			TOTAL MILES	
		From	To	Start	End	Distance (km)	Business	Private

Daily checks	Tires/Wheel	Wipers	Lights	Mirrors	Horn	Seatbelts	Brakes	Coupling devices
Monday								
Tuesday								
Wednesday								
Thursday								
Friday								
Saturday								
Sunday								

Fuel Input				
Date	Quantity	Unit	Mileage	Units

Notes :

Signature :

Vehicle Mileage Logbook

Sheet no.:

Make : Model : Year : License number :

DATE	PURPOSE OF TRAVEL	JOURNEY		ODOMETER READING			TOTAL MILES	
		From	To	Start	End	Distance (km)	Business	Private

Daily checks	Tires/Wheel	Wipers	Lights	Mirrors	Horn	Seatbelts	Brakes	Coupling devices
Monday								
Tuesday								
Wednesday								
Thursday								
Friday								
Saturday								
Sunday								

Fuel Input				
Date	Quantity	Unit	Mileage	Units

Notes :

Signature :

Vehicle Mileage Logbook

Sheet no.:

Make : Model : Year : License number :

DATE	PURPOSE OF TRAVEL	JOURNEY		ODOMETER READING			TOTAL MILES	
		From	To	Start	End	Distance (km)	Business	Private

Daily checks	Tires/Wheel	Wipers	Lights	Mirrors	Horn	Seatbelts	Brakes	Coupling devices
Monday								
Tuesday								
Wednesday								
Thursday								
Friday								
Saturday								
Sunday								

Fuel Input				
Date	Quantity	Unit	Mileage	Units

Notes :

Signature :

Vehicle Mileage Logbook

Sheet no.:

Make :   Model :   Year :   License number :

DATE	PURPOSE OF TRAVEL	JOURNEY		ODOMETER READING			TOTAL MILES	
		From	To	Start	End	Distance (km)	Business	Private

Daily checks	Tires/Wheel	Wipers	Lights	Mirrors	Horn	Seatbelts	Brakes	Coupling devices
Monday								
Tuesday								
Wednesday								
Thursday								
Friday								
Saturday								
Sunday								

Fuel Input				
Date	Quantity	Unit	Mileage	Units

Notes :

Signature :

Vehicle Mileage Logbook

Sheet no.:

Make :   Model :   Year :   License number :

DATE	PURPOSE OF TRAVEL	JOURNEY		ODOMETER READING			TOTAL MILES	
		From	To	Start	End	Distance (km)	Business	Private

Daily checks	Tires/Wheel	Wipers	Lights	Mirrors	Horn	Seatbelts	Brakes	Coupling devices
Monday								
Tuesday								
Wednesday								
Thursday								
Friday								
Saturday								
Sunday								

Fuel Input				
Date	Quantity	Unit	Mileage	Units

Notes :

Signature :

Vehicle Mileage Logbook

Sheet no.:

Make :　　　　Model :　　　　Year :　　　　License number :

DATE	PURPOSE OF TRAVEL	JOURNEY		ODOMETER READING			TOTAL MILES	
		From	To	Start	End	Distance (km)	Business	Private

Daily checks	Tires/Wheel	Wipers	Lights	Mirrors	Horn	Seatbelts	Brakes	Coupling devices
Monday								
Tuesday								
Wednesday								
Thursday								
Friday								
Saturday								
Sunday								

Fuel Input				
Date	Quantity	Unit	Mileage	Units

Notes :

Signature :

Vehicle Mileage Logbook

Sheet no.:

Make :   Model :   Year :   License number :

DATE	PURPOSE OF TRAVEL	JOURNEY		ODOMETER READING			TOTAL MILES	
		From	To	Start	End	Distance (km)	Business	Private

Daily checks	Tires/Wheel	Wipers	Lights	Mirrors	Horn	Seatbelts	Brakes	Coupling devices
Monday								
Tuesday								
Wednesday								
Thursday								
Friday								
Saturday								
Sunday								

Fuel Input

Date	Quantity	Unit	Mileage	Units

Notes :

Signature :

Vehicle Mileage Logbook

Sheet no.:

Make :　　Model :　　Year :　　License number :

DATE	PURPOSE OF TRAVEL	JOURNEY		ODOMETER READING			TOTAL MILES	
		From	To	Start	End	Distance (km)	Business	Private

Daily checks	Tires/Wheel	Wipers	Lights	Mirrors	Horn	Seatbelts	Brakes	Coupling devices
Monday								
Tuesday								
Wednesday								
Thursday								
Friday								
Saturday								
Sunday								

Fuel Input				
Date	Quantity	Unit	Mileage	Units

Notes :

Signature :

Vehicle Mileage Logbook

Sheet no.:

Make : Model : Year : License number :

DATE	PURPOSE OF TRAVEL	JOURNEY		ODOMETER READING			TOTAL MILES	
		From	To	Start	End	Distance (km)	Business	Private

Daily checks	Tires/Wheel	Wipers	Lights	Mirrors	Horn	Seatbelts	Brakes	Coupling devices
Monday								
Tuesday								
Wednesday								
Thursday								
Friday								
Saturday								
Sunday								

Fuel Input				
Date	Quantity	Unit	Mileage	Units

Notes :

Signature :

Vehicle Mileage Logbook

Sheet no.:

Make :　　　　Model :　　　　Year :　　　　License number :

DATE	PURPOSE OF TRAVEL	JOURNEY		ODOMETER READING			TOTAL MILES	
		From	To	Start	End	Distance (km)	Business	Private

Daily checks	Tires/Wheel	Wipers	Lights	Mirrors	Horn	Seatbelts	Brakes	Coupling devices
Monday								
Tuesday								
Wednesday								
Thursday								
Friday								
Saturday								
Sunday								

Fuel Input				
Date	Quantity	Unit	Mileage	Units

Notes :

Signature :

Vehicle Mileage Logbook

Sheet no.:

Make : Model : Year : License number :

DATE	PURPOSE OF TRAVEL	JOURNEY		ODOMETER READING			TOTAL MILES	
		From	To	Start	End	Distance (km)	Business	Private

Daily checks	Tires/Wheel	Wipers	Lights	Mirrors	Horn	Seatbelts	Brakes	Coupling devices
Monday								
Tuesday								
Wednesday								
Thursday								
Friday								
Saturday								
Sunday								

Fuel Input				
Date	Quantity	Unit	Mileage	Units

Notes :

Signature :

Vehicle Mileage Logbook

Sheet no.:

Make :   Model :   Year :   License number :

DATE	PURPOSE OF TRAVEL	JOURNEY		ODOMETER READING			TOTAL MILES	
		From	To	Start	End	Distance (km)	Business	Private

Daily checks	Tires/Wheel	Wipers	Lights	Mirrors	Horn	Seatbelts	Brakes	Coupling devices
Monday								
Tuesday								
Wednesday								
Thursday								
Friday								
Saturday								
Sunday								

Fuel Input

Date	Quantity	Unit	Mileage	Units

Notes :

Signature :

Vehicle Mileage Logbook

Sheet no.:

Make : Model : Year : License number :

DATE	PURPOSE OF TRAVEL	JOURNEY		ODOMETER READING			TOTAL MILES	
		From	To	Start	End	Distance (km)	Business	Private

Daily checks	Tires/ Wheel	Wipers	Lights	Mirrors	Horn	Seatbelts	Brakes	Coupling devices
Monday								
Tuesday								
Wednesday								
Thursday								
Friday								
Saturday								
Sunday								

Fuel Input				
Date	Quantity	Unit	Mileage	Units

Notes :

Signature :

Vehicle Mileage Logbook

Sheet no.:

Make : Model : Year : License number :

DATE	PURPOSE OF TRAVEL	JOURNEY		ODOMETER READING			TOTAL MILES	
		From	To	Start	End	Distance (km)	Business	Private

Daily checks	Tires/Wheel	Wipers	Lights	Mirrors	Horn	Seatbelts	Brakes	Coupling devices
Monday								
Tuesday								
Wednesday								
Thursday								
Friday								
Saturday								
Sunday								

Fuel Input				
Date	Quantity	Unit	Mileage	Units

Notes :

Signature :

Vehicle Mileage Logbook

Sheet no.:

Make : Model : Year : License number :

DATE	PURPOSE OF TRAVEL	JOURNEY		ODOMETER READING			TOTAL MILES	
		From	To	Start	End	Distance (km)	Business	Private

Daily checks	Tires/Wheel	Wipers	Lights	Mirrors	Horn	Seatbelts	Brakes	Coupling devices
Monday								
Tuesday								
Wednesday								
Thursday								
Friday								
Saturday								
Sunday								

Fuel Input				
Date	Quantity	Unit	Mileage	Units

Notes :

Signature :

Vehicle Mileage Logbook

Sheet no.:

Make :　　　Model :　　　Year :　　　License number :

DATE	PURPOSE OF TRAVEL	JOURNEY		ODOMETER READING			TOTAL MILES	
		From	To	Start	End	Distance (km)	Business	Private

Daily checks	Tires/Wheel	Wipers	Lights	Mirrors	Horn	Seatbelts	Brakes	Coupling devices
Monday								
Tuesday								
Wednesday								
Thursday								
Friday								
Saturday								
Sunday								

Fuel Input

Date	Quantity	Unit	Mileage	Units

Notes :

Signature :

Vehicle Mileage Logbook

Sheet no.:

Make : Model : Year : License number :

DATE	PURPOSE OF TRAVEL	JOURNEY		ODOMETER READING			TOTAL MILES	
		From	To	Start	End	Distance (km)	Business	Private

Daily checks	Tires/Wheel	Wipers	Lights	Mirrors	Horn	Seatbelts	Brakes	Coupling devices
Monday								
Tuesday								
Wednesday								
Thursday								
Friday								
Saturday								
Sunday								

Fuel Input				
Date	Quantity	Unit	Mileage	Units

Notes :

Signature :

Vehicle Mileage Logbook

Sheet no.:

Make :　　　Model :　　　Year :　　　License number :

DATE	PURPOSE OF TRAVEL	JOURNEY		ODOMETER READING			TOTAL MILES	
		From	To	Start	End	Distance (km)	Business	Private

Daily checks	Tires/Wheel	Wipers	Lights	Mirrors	Horn	Seatbelts	Brakes	Coupling devices
Monday								
Tuesday								
Wednesday								
Thursday								
Friday								
Saturday								
Sunday								

Fuel Input				
Date	Quantity	Unit	Mileage	Units

Notes :

Signature :

Vehicle Mileage Logbook

Sheet no.:

Make :   Model :   Year :   License number :

DATE	PURPOSE OF TRAVEL	JOURNEY		ODOMETER READING			TOTAL MILES	
		From	To	Start	End	Distance (km)	Business	Private

Daily checks	Tires/Wheel	Wipers	Lights	Mirrors	Horn	Seatbelts	Brakes	Coupling devices
Monday								
Tuesday								
Wednesday								
Thursday								
Friday								
Saturday								
Sunday								

Fuel Input				
Date	Quantity	Unit	Mileage	Units

Notes :

Signature :

Vehicle Mileage Logbook

Sheet no.:

Make : Model : Year : License number :

DATE	PURPOSE OF TRAVEL	JOURNEY		ODOMETER READING			TOTAL MILES	
		From	To	Start	End	Distance (km)	Business	Private

Daily checks	Tires/Wheel	Wipers	Lights	Mirrors	Horn	Seatbelts	Brakes	Coupling devices
Monday								
Tuesday								
Wednesday								
Thursday								
Friday								
Saturday								
Sunday								

Fuel Input

Date	Quantity	Unit	Mileage	Units

Notes :

Signature :

Vehicle Mileage Logbook

Sheet no.:

Make :   Model :   Year :   License number :

DATE	PURPOSE OF TRAVEL	JOURNEY		ODOMETER READING			TOTAL MILES	
		From	To	Start	End	Distance (km)	Business	Private

Daily checks	Tires/Wheel	Wipers	Lights	Mirrors	Horn	Seatbelts	Brakes	Coupling devices
Monday								
Tuesday								
Wednesday								
Thursday								
Friday								
Saturday								
Sunday								

Fuel Input				
Date	Quantity	Unit	Mileage	Units

Notes :

Signature :

Vehicle Mileage Logbook

Sheet no.:

Make : Model : Year : License number :

DATE	PURPOSE OF TRAVEL	JOURNEY		ODOMETER READING			TOTAL MILES	
		From	To	Start	End	Distance (km)	Business	Private

Daily checks	Tires/Wheel	Wipers	Lights	Mirrors	Horn	Seatbelts	Brakes	Coupling devices
Monday								
Tuesday								
Wednesday								
Thursday								
Friday								
Saturday								
Sunday								

Fuel Input				
Date	Quantity	Unit	Mileage	Units

Notes :

Signature :

Vehicle Mileage Logbook

Sheet no.:

Make : Model : Year : License number :

DATE	PURPOSE OF TRAVEL	JOURNEY		ODOMETER READING			TOTAL MILES	
		From	To	Start	End	Distance (km)	Business	Private

Daily checks	Tires/Wheel	Wipers	Lights	Mirrors	Horn	Seatbelts	Brakes	Coupling devices
Monday								
Tuesday								
Wednesday								
Thursday								
Friday								
Saturday								
Sunday								

Fuel Input				
Date	Quantity	Unit	Mileage	Units

Notes :

Signature :

Vehicle Mileage Logbook

Sheet no.:

Make :　　　Model :　　　Year :　　　License number :

DATE	PURPOSE OF TRAVEL	JOURNEY		ODOMETER READING			TOTAL MILES	
		From	To	Start	End	Distance (km)	Business	Private

Daily checks	Tires/Wheel	Wipers	Lights	Mirrors	Horn	Seatbelts	Brakes	Coupling devices
Monday								
Tuesday								
Wednesday								
Thursday								
Friday								
Saturday								
Sunday								

Fuel Input				
Date	Quantity	Unit	Mileage	Units

Notes :

Signature :

Vehicle Mileage Logbook

Sheet no.:

Make :   Model :   Year :   License number :

DATE	PURPOSE OF TRAVEL	JOURNEY		ODOMETER READING			TOTAL MILES	
		From	To	Start	End	Distance (km)	Business	Private

Daily checks	Tires/Wheel	Wipers	Lights	Mirrors	Horn	Seatbelts	Brakes	Coupling devices
Monday								
Tuesday								
Wednesday								
Thursday								
Friday								
Saturday								
Sunday								

Fuel Input				
Date	Quantity	Unit	Mileage	Units

Notes :

Signature :

Vehicle Mileage Logbook

Sheet no.:

Make : Model : Year : License number :

DATE	PURPOSE OF TRAVEL	JOURNEY		ODOMETER READING			TOTAL MILES	
		From	To	Start	End	Distance (km)	Business	Private

Daily checks	Tires/ Wheel	Wipers	Lights	Mirrors	Horn	Seatbelts	Brakes	Coupling devices
Monday								
Tuesday								
Wednesday								
Thursday								
Friday								
Saturday								
Sunday								

Fuel Input				
Date	Quantity	Unit	Mileage	Units

Notes :

Signature :

Vehicle Mileage Logbook

Sheet no.:

Make :   Model :   Year :   License number :

DATE	PURPOSE OF TRAVEL	JOURNEY		ODOMETER READING			TOTAL MILES	
		From	To	Start	End	Distance (km)	Business	Private

Daily checks	Tires/Wheel	Wipers	Lights	Mirrors	Horn	Seatbelts	Brakes	Coupling devices
Monday								
Tuesday								
Wednesday								
Thursday								
Friday								
Saturday								
Sunday								

Fuel Input				
Date	Quantity	Unit	Mileage	Units

Notes :

Signature :

Vehicle Mileage Logbook

Sheet no.:

Make :   Model :   Year :   License number :

DATE	PURPOSE OF TRAVEL	JOURNEY		ODOMETER READING			TOTAL MILES	
		From	To	Start	End	Distance (km)	Business	Private

Daily checks	Tires/Wheel	Wipers	Lights	Mirrors	Horn	Seatbelts	Brakes	Coupling devices
Monday								
Tuesday								
Wednesday								
Thursday								
Friday								
Saturday								
Sunday								

Fuel Input				
Date	Quantity	Unit	Mileage	Units

Notes :

Signature :

Vehicle Mileage Logbook

Sheet no.:

Make :　　　Model :　　　Year :　　　License number :

DATE	PURPOSE OF TRAVEL	JOURNEY		ODOMETER READING			TOTAL MILES	
		From	To	Start	End	Distance (km)	Business	Private

Daily checks	Tires/Wheel	Wipers	Lights	Mirrors	Horn	Seatbelts	Brakes	Coupling devices
Monday								
Tuesday								
Wednesday								
Thursday								
Friday								
Saturday								
Sunday								

Fuel Input				
Date	Quantity	Unit	Mileage	Units

Notes :

Signature :

Vehicle Mileage Logbook

Sheet no.:

Make :   Model :   Year :   License number :

DATE	PURPOSE OF TRAVEL	JOURNEY		ODOMETER READING			TOTAL MILES	
		From	To	Start	End	Distance (km)	Business	Private

Daily checks	Tires/Wheel	Wipers	Lights	Mirrors	Horn	Seatbelts	Brakes	Coupling devices
Monday								
Tuesday								
Wednesday								
Thursday								
Friday								
Saturday								
Sunday								

Fuel Input				
Date	Quantity	Unit	Mileage	Units

Notes :

Signature :

Vehicle Mileage Logbook

Sheet no.:

Make : Model : Year : License number :

DATE	PURPOSE OF TRAVEL	JOURNEY		ODOMETER READING			TOTAL MILES	
		From	To	Start	End	Distance (km)	Business	Private

Daily checks	Tires/Wheel	Wipers	Lights	Mirrors	Horn	Seatbelts	Brakes	Coupling devices
Monday								
Tuesday								
Wednesday								
Thursday								
Friday								
Saturday								
Sunday								

Fuel Input				
Date	Quantity	Unit	Mileage	Units

Notes :

Signature :

Vehicle Mileage Logbook

Sheet no.:

Make : Model : Year : License number :

DATE	PURPOSE OF TRAVEL	JOURNEY		ODOMETER READING			TOTAL MILES	
		From	To	Start	End	Distance (km)	Business	Private

Daily checks	Tires/Wheel	Wipers	Lights	Mirrors	Horn	Seatbelts	Brakes	Coupling devices
Monday								
Tuesday								
Wednesday								
Thursday								
Friday								
Saturday								
Sunday								

Fuel Input				
Date	Quantity	Unit	Mileage	Units

Notes :

Signature :

Vehicle Mileage Logbook

Sheet no.:

Make : Model : Year : License number :

DATE	PURPOSE OF TRAVEL	JOURNEY		ODOMETER READING			TOTAL MILES	
		From	To	Start	End	Distance (km)	Business	Private

Daily checks	Tires/Wheel	Wipers	Lights	Mirrors	Horn	Seatbelts	Brakes	Coupling devices
Monday								
Tuesday								
Wednesday								
Thursday								
Friday								
Saturday								
Sunday								

Fuel Input				
Date	Quantity	Unit	Mileage	Units

Notes :

Signature :

Vehicle Mileage Logbook

Sheet no.:

Make :   Model :   Year :   License number :

DATE	PURPOSE OF TRAVEL	JOURNEY		ODOMETER READING			TOTAL MILES	
		From	To	Start	End	Distance (km)	Business	Private

Daily checks	Tires/Wheel	Wipers	Lights	Mirrors	Horn	Seatbelts	Brakes	Coupling devices
Monday								
Tuesday								
Wednesday								
Thursday								
Friday								
Saturday								
Sunday								

Fuel Input				
Date	Quantity	Unit	Mileage	Units

Notes :

Signature :

Vehicle Mileage Logbook

Sheet no.:

Make : Model : Year : License number :

DATE	PURPOSE OF TRAVEL	JOURNEY		ODOMETER READING			TOTAL MILES	
		From	To	Start	End	Distance (km)	Business	Private

Daily checks	Tires/ Wheel	Wipers	Lights	Mirrors	Horn	Seatbelts	Brakes	Coupling devices
Monday								
Tuesday								
Wednesday								
Thursday								
Friday								
Saturday								
Sunday								

Fuel Input				
Date	Quantity	Unit	Mileage	Units

Notes :

Signature :

Vehicle Mileage Logbook

Sheet no.:

Make :   Model :   Year :   License number :

DATE	PURPOSE OF TRAVEL	JOURNEY		ODOMETER READING			TOTAL MILES	
		From	To	Start	End	Distance (km)	Business	Private

Daily checks	Tires/Wheel	Wipers	Lights	Mirrors	Horn	Seatbelts	Brakes	Coupling devices
Monday								
Tuesday								
Wednesday								
Thursday								
Friday								
Saturday								
Sunday								

Fuel Input				
Date	Quantity	Unit	Mileage	Units

Notes :

Signature :

Vehicle Mileage Logbook

Sheet no.:

Make :　　　　Model :　　　　Year :　　　　License number :

DATE	PURPOSE OF TRAVEL	JOURNEY		ODOMETER READING			TOTAL MILES	
		From	To	Start	End	Distance (km)	Business	Private

Daily checks	Tires/Wheel	Wipers	Lights	Mirrors	Horn	Seatbelts	Brakes	Coupling devices
Monday								
Tuesday								
Wednesday								
Thursday								
Friday								
Saturday								
Sunday								

Fuel Input				
Date	Quantity	Unit	Mileage	Units

Notes :

Signature :

Vehicle Mileage Logbook

Sheet no.:

Make : Model : Year : License number :

DATE	PURPOSE OF TRAVEL	JOURNEY		ODOMETER READING			TOTAL MILES	
		From	To	Start	End	Distance (km)	Business	Private

Daily checks	Tires/Wheel	Wipers	Lights	Mirrors	Horn	Seatbelts	Brakes	Coupling devices
Monday								
Tuesday								
Wednesday								
Thursday								
Friday								
Saturday								
Sunday								

Fuel Input				
Date	Quantity	Unit	Mileage	Units

Notes :

Signature :

Vehicle Mileage Logbook

Sheet no.:

Make : Model : Year : License number :

DATE	PURPOSE OF TRAVEL	JOURNEY		ODOMETER READING			TOTAL MILES	
		From	To	Start	End	Distance (km)	Business	Private

Daily checks	Tires/Wheel	Wipers	Lights	Mirrors	Horn	Seatbelts	Brakes	Coupling devices
Monday								
Tuesday								
Wednesday								
Thursday								
Friday								
Saturday								
Sunday								

Fuel Input				
Date	Quantity	Unit	Mileage	Units

Notes :

Signature :

Vehicle Mileage Logbook

Sheet no.:

Make :   Model :   Year :   License number :

DATE	PURPOSE OF TRAVEL	JOURNEY		ODOMETER READING			TOTAL MILES	
		From	To	Start	End	Distance (km)	Business	Private

Daily checks	Tires/ Wheel	Wipers	Lights	Mirrors	Horn	Seatbelts	Brakes	Coupling devices
Monday								
Tuesday								
Wednesday								
Thursday								
Friday								
Saturday								
Sunday								

Fuel Input				
Date	Quantity	Unit	Mileage	Units

Notes :

Signature :

Vehicle Mileage Logbook

Sheet no.:

Make :　　　　Model :　　　　Year :　　　　License number :

DATE	PURPOSE OF TRAVEL	JOURNEY		ODOMETER READING			TOTAL MILES	
		From	To	Start	End	Distance (km)	Business	Private

Daily checks	Tires/Wheel	Wipers	Lights	Mirrors	Horn	Seatbelts	Brakes	Coupling devices
Monday								
Tuesday								
Wednesday								
Thursday								
Friday								
Saturday								
Sunday								

Fuel Input

Date	Quantity	Unit	Mileage	Units

Notes :

Signature :

Vehicle Mileage Logbook

Sheet no.:

Make :　　　　Model :　　　　Year :　　　　License number :

DATE	PURPOSE OF TRAVEL	JOURNEY		ODOMETER READING			TOTAL MILES	
		From	To	Start	End	Distance (km)	Business	Private

Daily checks	Tires/Wheel	Wipers	Lights	Mirrors	Horn	Seatbelts	Brakes	Coupling devices
Monday								
Tuesday								
Wednesday								
Thursday								
Friday								
Saturday								
Sunday								

Fuel Input				
Date	Quantity	Unit	Mileage	Units

Notes :

Signature :

Vehicle Mileage Logbook

Sheet no.:

Make : Model : Year : License number :

DATE	PURPOSE OF TRAVEL	JOURNEY		ODOMETER READING			TOTAL MILES	
		From	To	Start	End	Distance (km)	Business	Private

Daily checks	Tires/Wheel	Wipers	Lights	Mirrors	Horn	Seatbelts	Brakes	Coupling devices
Monday								
Tuesday								
Wednesday								
Thursday								
Friday								
Saturday								
Sunday								

Fuel Input

Date	Quantity	Unit	Mileage	Units

Notes :

Signature :

Vehicle Mileage Logbook

Sheet no.:

Make :   Model :   Year :   License number :

DATE	PURPOSE OF TRAVEL	JOURNEY		ODOMETER READING			TOTAL MILES	
		From	To	Start	End	Distance (km)	Business	Private

Daily checks	Tires/Wheel	Wipers	Lights	Mirrors	Horn	Seatbelts	Brakes	Coupling devices
Monday								
Tuesday								
Wednesday								
Thursday								
Friday								
Saturday								
Sunday								

Fuel Input

Date	Quantity	Unit	Mileage	Units

Notes :

Signature :

Vehicle Mileage Logbook

Sheet no.:

Make :   Model :   Year :   License number :

DATE	PURPOSE OF TRAVEL	JOURNEY		ODOMETER READING			TOTAL MILES	
		From	To	Start	End	Distance (km)	Business	Private

Daily checks	Tires/Wheel	Wipers	Lights	Mirrors	Horn	Seatbelts	Brakes	Coupling devices
Monday								
Tuesday								
Wednesday								
Thursday								
Friday								
Saturday								
Sunday								

Fuel Input				
Date	Quantity	Unit	Mileage	Units

Notes :

Signature :

Vehicle Mileage Logbook

Sheet no.:

Make : Model : Year : License number :

DATE	PURPOSE OF TRAVEL	JOURNEY		ODOMETER READING			TOTAL MILES	
		From	To	Start	End	Distance (km)	Business	Private

Daily checks	Tires/Wheel	Wipers	Lights	Mirrors	Horn	Seatbelts	Brakes	Coupling devices
Monday								
Tuesday								
Wednesday								
Thursday								
Friday								
Saturday								
Sunday								

Fuel Input				
Date	Quantity	Unit	Mileage	Units

Notes :

Signature :

Vehicle Mileage Logbook

Sheet no.:

Make :   Model :   Year :   License number :

DATE	PURPOSE OF TRAVEL	JOURNEY		ODOMETER READING			TOTAL MILES	
		From	To	Start	End	Distance (km)	Business	Private

Daily checks	Tires/Wheel	Wipers	Lights	Mirrors	Horn	Seatbelts	Brakes	Coupling devices
Monday								
Tuesday								
Wednesday								
Thursday								
Friday								
Saturday								
Sunday								

Fuel Input				
Date	Quantity	Unit	Mileage	Units

Notes :

Signature :

Vehicle Mileage Logbook

Sheet no.:

Make :   Model :   Year :   License number :

DATE	PURPOSE OF TRAVEL	JOURNEY		ODOMETER READING			TOTAL MILES	
		From	To	Start	End	Distance (km)	Business	Private

Daily checks	Tires/Wheel	Wipers	Lights	Mirrors	Horn	Seatbelts	Brakes	Coupling devices
Monday								
Tuesday								
Wednesday								
Thursday								
Friday								
Saturday								
Sunday								

Fuel Input				
Date	Quantity	Unit	Mileage	Units

Notes :

Signature :

Vehicle Mileage Logbook

Sheet no.:

Make : Model : Year : License number :

DATE	PURPOSE OF TRAVEL	JOURNEY		ODOMETER READING			TOTAL MILES	
		From	To	Start	End	Distance (km)	Business	Private

Daily checks	Tires/Wheel	Wipers	Lights	Mirrors	Horn	Seatbelts	Brakes	Coupling devices
Monday								
Tuesday								
Wednesday								
Thursday								
Friday								
Saturday								
Sunday								

Fuel Input				
Date	Quantity	Unit	Mileage	Units

Notes :

Signature :

Vehicle Mileage Logbook

Sheet no.:

Make :   Model :   Year :   License number :

DATE	PURPOSE OF TRAVEL	JOURNEY		ODOMETER READING			TOTAL MILES	
		From	To	Start	End	Distance (km)	Business	Private

Daily checks	Tires/Wheel	Wipers	Lights	Mirrors	Horn	Seatbelts	Brakes	Coupling devices
Monday								
Tuesday								
Wednesday								
Thursday								
Friday								
Saturday								
Sunday								

Fuel Input				
Date	Quantity	Unit	Mileage	Units

Notes :

Signature :

Vehicle Mileage Logbook

Sheet no.:

Make : Model : Year : License number :

DATE	PURPOSE OF TRAVEL	JOURNEY		ODOMETER READING			TOTAL MILES	
		From	To	Start	End	Distance (km)	Business	Private

Daily checks	Tires/Wheel	Wipers	Lights	Mirrors	Horn	Seatbelts	Brakes	Coupling devices
Monday								
Tuesday								
Wednesday								
Thursday								
Friday								
Saturday								
Sunday								

Fuel Input				
Date	Quantity	Unit	Mileage	Units

Notes :

Signature :

Vehicle Mileage Logbook

Sheet no.:

Make : Model : Year : License number :

DATE	PURPOSE OF TRAVEL	JOURNEY		ODOMETER READING			TOTAL MILES	
		From	To	Start	End	Distance (km)	Business	Private

Daily checks	Tires/Wheel	Wipers	Lights	Mirrors	Horn	Seatbelts	Brakes	Coupling devices
Monday								
Tuesday								
Wednesday								
Thursday								
Friday								
Saturday								
Sunday								

Fuel Input

Date	Quantity	Unit	Mileage	Units

Notes :

Signature :

Vehicle Mileage Logbook

Sheet no.:

Make :　　Model :　　Year :　　License number :

DATE	PURPOSE OF TRAVEL	JOURNEY		ODOMETER READING			TOTAL MILES	
		From	To	Start	End	Distance (km)	Business	Private

Daily checks	Tires/Wheel	Wipers	Lights	Mirrors	Horn	Seatbelts	Brakes	Coupling devices
Monday								
Tuesday								
Wednesday								
Thursday								
Friday								
Saturday								
Sunday								

Fuel Input				
Date	Quantity	Unit	Mileage	Units

Notes :

Signature :

Vehicle Mileage Logbook

Sheet no.:

Make :   Model :   Year :   License number :

DATE	PURPOSE OF TRAVEL	JOURNEY		ODOMETER READING			TOTAL MILES	
		From	To	Start	End	Distance (km)	Business	Private

Daily checks	Tires/Wheel	Wipers	Lights	Mirrors	Horn	Seatbelts	Brakes	Coupling devices
Monday								
Tuesday								
Wednesday								
Thursday								
Friday								
Saturday								
Sunday								

Fuel Input				
Date	Quantity	Unit	Mileage	Units

Notes :

Signature :

Vehicle Mileage Logbook

Sheet no.:

Make :   Model :   Year :   License number :

DATE	PURPOSE OF TRAVEL	JOURNEY		ODOMETER READING			TOTAL MILES	
		From	To	Start	End	Distance (km)	Business	Private

Daily checks	Tires/Wheel	Wipers	Lights	Mirrors	Horn	Seatbelts	Brakes	Coupling devices
Monday								
Tuesday								
Wednesday								
Thursday								
Friday								
Saturday								
Sunday								

Fuel Input				
Date	Quantity	Unit	Mileage	Units

Notes :

Signature :

Vehicle Mileage Logbook

Sheet no.:

Make :　　　　Model :　　　　Year :　　　　License number :

DATE	PURPOSE OF TRAVEL	JOURNEY		ODOMETER READING			TOTAL MILES	
		From	To	Start	End	Distance (km)	Business	Private

Daily checks	Tires/ Wheel	Wipers	Lights	Mirrors	Horn	Seatbelts	Brakes	Coupling devices
Monday								
Tuesday								
Wednesday								
Thursday								
Friday								
Saturday								
Sunday								

Fuel Input				
Date	Quantity	Unit	Mileage	Units

Notes :

Signature :

Vehicle Mileage Logbook

Sheet no.:

Make :　　　　Model :　　　　Year :　　　　License number :

DATE	PURPOSE OF TRAVEL	JOURNEY		ODOMETER READING			TOTAL MILES	
		From	To	Start	End	Distance (km)	Business	Private

Daily checks	Tires/Wheel	Wipers	Lights	Mirrors	Horn	Seatbelts	Brakes	Coupling devices
Monday								
Tuesday								
Wednesday								
Thursday								
Friday								
Saturday								
Sunday								

Fuel Input

Date	Quantity	Unit	Mileage	Units

Notes :

Signature :

Vehicle Mileage Logbook

Sheet no.:

Make : Model : Year : License number :

DATE	PURPOSE OF TRAVEL	JOURNEY		ODOMETER READING			TOTAL MILES	
		From	To	Start	End	Distance (km)	Business	Private

Daily checks	Tires/Wheel	Wipers	Lights	Mirrors	Horn	Seatbelts	Brakes	Coupling devices
Monday								
Tuesday								
Wednesday								
Thursday								
Friday								
Saturday								
Sunday								

Fuel Input				
Date	Quantity	Unit	Mileage	Units

Notes :

Signature :

Vehicle Mileage Logbook

Sheet no.:

Make : Model : Year : License number :

DATE	PURPOSE OF TRAVEL	JOURNEY		ODOMETER READING			TOTAL MILES	
		From	To	Start	End	Distance (km)	Business	Private

Daily checks	Tires/Wheel	Wipers	Lights	Mirrors	Horn	Seatbelts	Brakes	Coupling devices
Monday								
Tuesday								
Wednesday								
Thursday								
Friday								
Saturday								
Sunday								

Fuel Input				
Date	Quantity	Unit	Mileage	Units

Notes :

Signature :

Vehicle Mileage Logbook

Sheet no.:

Make : Model : Year : License number :

DATE	PURPOSE OF TRAVEL	JOURNEY		ODOMETER READING			TOTAL MILES	
		From	To	Start	End	Distance (km)	Business	Private

Daily checks	Tires/Wheel	Wipers	Lights	Mirrors	Horn	Seatbelts	Brakes	Coupling devices
Monday								
Tuesday								
Wednesday								
Thursday								
Friday								
Saturday								
Sunday								

Fuel Input

Date	Quantity	Unit	Mileage	Units

Notes :

Signature :

Vehicle Mileage Logbook

Sheet no.:

Make : Model : Year : License number :

DATE	PURPOSE OF TRAVEL	JOURNEY		ODOMETER READING			TOTAL MILES	
		From	To	Start	End	Distance (km)	Business	Private

Daily checks	Tires/ Wheel	Wipers	Lights	Mirrors	Horn	Seatbelts	Brakes	Coupling devices
Monday								
Tuesday								
Wednesday								
Thursday								
Friday								
Saturday								
Sunday								

Fuel Input				
Date	Quantity	Unit	Mileage	Units

Notes :

Signature :

Vehicle Mileage Logbook

Sheet no.:

Make :   Model :   Year :   License number :

DATE	PURPOSE OF TRAVEL	JOURNEY		ODOMETER READING			TOTAL MILES	
		From	To	Start	End	Distance (km)	Business	Private

Daily checks	Tires/Wheel	Wipers	Lights	Mirrors	Horn	Seatbelts	Brakes	Coupling devices
Monday								
Tuesday								
Wednesday								
Thursday								
Friday								
Saturday								
Sunday								

Fuel Input				
Date	Quantity	Unit	Mileage	Units

Notes :

Signature :

Vehicle Mileage Logbook

Sheet no.:

Make :   Model :   Year :   License number :

DATE	PURPOSE OF TRAVEL	JOURNEY		ODOMETER READING			TOTAL MILES	
		From	To	Start	End	Distance (km)	Business	Private

Daily checks	Tires/Wheel	Wipers	Lights	Mirrors	Horn	Seatbelts	Brakes	Coupling devices
Monday								
Tuesday								
Wednesday								
Thursday								
Friday								
Saturday								
Sunday								

Fuel Input				
Date	Quantity	Unit	Mileage	Units

Notes :

Signature :

Vehicle Mileage Logbook

Sheet no.:

Make :   Model :   Year :   License number :

DATE	PURPOSE OF TRAVEL	JOURNEY		ODOMETER READING			TOTAL MILES	
		From	To	Start	End	Distance (km)	Business	Private

Daily checks	Tires/Wheel	Wipers	Lights	Mirrors	Horn	Seatbelts	Brakes	Coupling devices
Monday								
Tuesday								
Wednesday								
Thursday								
Friday								
Saturday								
Sunday								

Fuel Input

Date	Quantity	Unit	Mileage	Units

Notes :

_____
_____
_____
_____
_____
_____
_____

Signature :

Vehicle Mileage Logbook

Sheet no.:

Make : Model : Year : License number :

DATE	PURPOSE OF TRAVEL	JOURNEY		ODOMETER READING			TOTAL MILES	
		From	To	Start	End	Distance (km)	Business	Private

Daily checks	Tires/Wheel	Wipers	Lights	Mirrors	Horn	Seatbelts	Brakes	Coupling devices
Monday								
Tuesday								
Wednesday								
Thursday								
Friday								
Saturday								
Sunday								

Fuel Input				
Date	Quantity	Unit	Mileage	Units

Notes :

Signature :

Vehicle Mileage Logbook

Sheet no.:

Make :　　　　Model :　　　　Year :　　　　License number :

DATE	PURPOSE OF TRAVEL	JOURNEY		ODOMETER READING			TOTAL MILES	
		From	To	Start	End	Distance (km)	Business	Private

Daily checks	Tires/Wheel	Wipers	Lights	Mirrors	Horn	Seatbelts	Brakes	Coupling devices
Monday								
Tuesday								
Wednesday								
Thursday								
Friday								
Saturday								
Sunday								

Fuel Input				
Date	Quantity	Unit	Mileage	Units

Notes :

Signature :

Vehicle Mileage Logbook

Sheet no.:

Make :   Model :   Year :   License number :

DATE	PURPOSE OF TRAVEL	JOURNEY		ODOMETER READING			TOTAL MILES	
		From	To	Start	End	Distance (km)	Business	Private

Daily checks	Tires/ Wheel	Wipers	Lights	Mirrors	Horn	Seatbelts	Brakes	Coupling devices
Monday								
Tuesday								
Wednesday								
Thursday								
Friday								
Saturday								
Sunday								

Fuel Input				
Date	Quantity	Unit	Mileage	Units

Notes :

Signature :

Vehicle Mileage Logbook

Sheet no.:

Make : Model : Year : License number :

DATE	PURPOSE OF TRAVEL	JOURNEY		ODOMETER READING			TOTAL MILES	
		From	To	Start	End	Distance (km)	Business	Private

Daily checks	Tires/Wheel	Wipers	Lights	Mirrors	Horn	Seatbelts	Brakes	Coupling devices
Monday								
Tuesday								
Wednesday								
Thursday								
Friday								
Saturday								
Sunday								

Fuel Input

Date	Quantity	Unit	Mileage	Units

Notes :

Signature :

Vehicle Mileage Logbook

Sheet no.:

Make :   Model :   Year :   License number :

DATE	PURPOSE OF TRAVEL	JOURNEY		ODOMETER READING			TOTAL MILES	
		From	To	Start	End	Distance (km)	Business	Private

Daily checks	Tires/Wheel	Wipers	Lights	Mirrors	Horn	Seatbelts	Brakes	Coupling devices
Monday								
Tuesday								
Wednesday								
Thursday								
Friday								
Saturday								
Sunday								

Fuel Input				
Date	Quantity	Unit	Mileage	Units

Notes :

Signature :

Vehicle Mileage Logbook

Sheet no.:

Make : Model : Year : License number :

DATE	PURPOSE OF TRAVEL	JOURNEY		ODOMETER READING			TOTAL MILES	
		From	To	Start	End	Distance (km)	Business	Private

Daily checks	Tires/Wheel	Wipers	Lights	Mirrors	Horn	Seatbelts	Brakes	Coupling devices
Monday								
Tuesday								
Wednesday								
Thursday								
Friday								
Saturday								
Sunday								

Fuel Input

Date	Quantity	Unit	Mileage	Units

Notes :

_____
_____
_____
_____
_____
_____

Signature :

Vehicle Mileage Logbook

Sheet no.:

Make :   Model :   Year :   License number :

DATE	PURPOSE OF TRAVEL	JOURNEY		ODOMETER READING			TOTAL MILES	
		From	To	Start	End	Distance (km)	Business	Private

Daily checks	Tires/Wheel	Wipers	Lights	Mirrors	Horn	Seatbelts	Brakes	Coupling devices
Monday								
Tuesday								
Wednesday								
Thursday								
Friday								
Saturday								
Sunday								

Fuel Input				
Date	Quantity	Unit	Mileage	Units

Notes :

Signature :

Vehicle Mileage Logbook

Sheet no.:

Make :   Model :   Year :   License number :

DATE	PURPOSE OF TRAVEL	JOURNEY		ODOMETER READING			TOTAL MILES	
		From	To	Start	End	Distance (km)	Business	Private

Daily checks	Tires/Wheel	Wipers	Lights	Mirrors	Horn	Seatbelts	Brakes	Coupling devices
Monday								
Tuesday								
Wednesday								
Thursday								
Friday								
Saturday								
Sunday								

Fuel Input				
Date	Quantity	Unit	Mileage	Units

Notes :

Signature :

Thank you!

WE ARE GLAD THAT YOU PURCHASED OUR BOOK!
PLEASE LET US KNOW HOW WE CAN IMPROVE IT!
YOUR FEEDBACK IS ESSENTIAL TO US.

Contact us at:

 log'Sin@gmail.com

JUST TITLE THE EMAIL 'CREATIVE' AND WE WILL GIVE YOU SOME EXTRA SURPRISES!

CPSIA information can be obtained
at www.ICGtesting.com
Printed in the USA
LVHW072344211122
733758LV00036B/1984